Double Your Dating

ONE STEP CLOSER TO LOVE

101 Tips To Find The One You've Been Looking For

STANLEY HALE

Table of Contents

Chapter 1: 6 Behaviours That Keep You Single 6
Chapter 2: 6 Ways To Have A Great First Date...10
Chapter 3: *6 Ways To Flirt With Someone* 15
Chapter 4: 5 DIFFERENCES BETWEEN CRUSHING AND FALLING IN LOVE...19
Chapter 5: 5 Signs Someone Only Likes You As A Friend..................22
Chapter 6: 8 Signs a Girl Likes You..25
Chapter 7: 6 Tips To Find The One..30
Chapter 8: Confidence: The Art of Humble-Pride......................................34
Chapter 9: *The Goal Is Not The Point* 36
Chapter 10: *Make Time for Your Partner* 39
Chapter 11: First Impressions Matter..42
Chapter 12: Don't Overthink Things 47
Chapter 13: Ten Signs Your Crush Likes You...49
Chapter 14: *The People You Need in Your Life* 55
Chapter 15: 5 Steps To Using Dating Apps Correctly.............................58
Chapter 16: *10 SIGNS HE DOESN'T LIKE YOU* 62
Chapter 17: How To Find Motivation 66
Chapter 18: 10 Facts About Attraction...72
Chapter 19: **Ten Ways Men Fall In Love** 76
Chapter 20: How To Not Live Your Life In Regret....................................82
Chapter 21: 10 TIPS TO STOP LIKING YOUR CRUSH 89
Chapter 22: 7 Signs You Have Found A Keeper...93
Chapter 23: Never Giving Up 97
Chapter 24: How to Love Yourself First 101
Chapter 25: *6 Relationship Goals To Have* 104
Chapter 26: 9 Signs an Introvert Likes You 108

Chapter 27: 6 Signs You Are Ready To Move To The Next Step In A Relationship 113

Chapter 1:
6 Behaviours That Keep You Single

Dating may not be as easy as it is shown in all those romantic Hollywood movies. There is so much more than appearance and stability in dating someone. And when you are old enough to be involved with someone, you sometimes find yourself uninterested. You think about how everyone your age has already started dating while you are back there eating junk and watching Netflix. It might appear to you that being in a relationship is tiresome, and you stop trying for it. Everyone has a different preference when it comes to finding someone for themselves. You tend to look for someone that matches your knight in the shining armor, which makes it hard for you to find someone you need.

Be true to you yourself while finding someone to date. Looking for someone with the expectation that you are rich and handsome would be foolish. It would be best if you worked on yourself more than that. Make yourself ease around with people but no so much that they start to get annoyed. Don't get in your way.

1. **Trust Is Essential**

Trusting each other is an important factor for dating someone. If you don't trust your partner even in the slightest, then nothing will matter. You will constantly doubt each other. Both of you will eventually fall apart if there is no trust. And if you have trust issues, it will be difficult for you to find someone worthy. But, if you trust too quickly, then it's only natural that you will break your bubble of expectations. Be friendly. Try to get to know them properly before making any assumptions about them. You don't want to go around hesitating about everything. Find yourself a reliable partner that trusts you too.

2. **Too Many Expectations**

Expecting too much from your partner will lead to only one thing. It leads towards Disappointment. It would help if you let them be. Don't expect things to go your way always. Your knight in the shining armor may be a bookworm because people find love in the most unexpected places. It doesn't always mean to keep no expectations at all. To keep the expectations low. You will get surprised constantly when you don't know what's coming your way. Don't let people cloud your judgment, and keep high standards about a relationship. Everyone has their share of ups and downs. Comparison with others will not be suitable for your relationship.

3. **Have Self-Confidence**

One has to respect itself before anything else can. You have to have self-esteem in you for people to take you seriously. It is true "you can't love someone unless you learn to love yourself first." You tend to feel insecure about yourself. Everything around you seems too perfect for you. And you constantly think that your partner will stop loving you one day. That fear of yours will get you nowhere. Try to give yourself as much care you can. It doesn't hurt to be loved.

4. **Don't Overthink**

You found a guy, and He seems to be excellent. But you start to overthink it. Eventually, you let go. That is what you shouldn't have done. Just try to go with the flow sometimes. Don't try too hard for it. Go for it the easy way. Overthinking will lead you to make up scenarios that never happened. Just let it be and see where it goes. Be easy so people can approach you. Think, don't overthink.

5. **Involving Too Many People**

When you initially start dating, you get nervous. People get help from their friends sometimes. But it is not necessary to get every move through them. Involving them in everything will only get your partner get uncomfortable and get you frustrated. People tend to give a lot of opinions of their own. You will get confused. So, it is good to keep these things to yourself. Be mindful in giving them a brief report from time to time. However, keep them at a reasonable distance.

6. **Giving Up Too Quickly**

If it doesn't work initially, it does not mean that it will never work. Patience is an essential element when it comes to dating anyone. Don't give up too quickly. Try to make it work until it's clear that it won't. Give it your all. Compromise on things you can. Because if both of you are not willing to compromise, it will not work between you both. It will work out in the end if it's meant to be. Don't push it if it's not working too.

Conclusion

It is hard; it keeps going at a pace. But all you must need is that spark that keeps it alive. Make it work until it doesn't. Go for it all. Make commitments only when you are sure about your choice. And be true to your words. Who wants to be single forever?

Chapter 2:
6 Ways To Have A Great First Date

Have you been crushing on someone hard for a long time and finally dared to ask them out? Well, congratulations that they've said yes! Or else why would you be here looking for ways to arrange a perfect date with them? Planning a good date can be nerve-wracking, especially if it's your first one and you have to make sure everything goes well and smoothly. You work hard on every detail so as to impress your date, and as the quote suggests, "the first impression is the last impression," you really are working on going the extra mile.

While you're hesitant that you need to plan a perfect date, you're also trying not to look too desperate or investing in something that may be won't work out. For example, if you have planned an expensive dinner in a luxurious restaurant but within minutes you realize that you don't click with your date, it will be pretty awkward for the both of you.

To help you with your anxieties, we have come up with some strategies and ways to make sure you have a great first date!

1. **Don't try to overcomplicate things:**

A first date is usually full of nervousness and uncertainty. There's a great chance that you know just a little about them, or maybe not at all. You have to make sure that you don't complicate things by making either very grand plans or keeping them to yourself for the whole day. Remember, you have to make them comfortable first, and these extravagant things definitely won't help with that. You can simply ask them out for a coffee or take them to watch a movie. This will help both you and your date decide if you want to spend more time with each other. If you both click well, a simple coffee in your local coffee shop will lead to lunch and dinner, or maybe more hangouts.

2. Get yourself into engaging conversations:

A personality would be rated 10/10 if the person has a deeper understanding and is intellectually clever. If you suffer from social anxiety or are quiet most of the time, you should prepare yourself with some intelligent topics beforehand to woo your date. Chances are, your date would most likely give you a poor score if you use cheesy pickup lines, lacking humor and empty compliments. It would be best if you tried telling an engaging story about your life that will impress your date instantly, and likewise, listen attentively to whatever the other person says about theirs. It would help if you practiced self-compassion before going, be confident enough that you're going to impress them. Having self-doubts and anxiety is expected before any significant event, but make sure it doesn't get to you.

3. Think about your past mistakes:

Have you been on several dates that ended up in disasters? And now you can't help but make sure this one doesn't end in the dumps too. For that, you have to use your power of memory flashbacks and relive every date you've been on. What was it that made your dates run away and not look back again? Maybe you weren't listening to them hard enough, or maybe your phone looked more of your date than the person sitting in Infront of you; perhaps you passed an unkind comment or hurt the other person's sentiments in some way, even if it was unintentional and you didn't realize it at that time. But it's okay. You should try and correct your mistakes instead of overthinking and dwelling on the negative stuff.

4. Different personalities could still be a perfect match:

If you're thinking, "Hey, I'm an engineer, and my date is a lawyer, I don't think we will click well," well then, you're clearly mistaken. You don't have to date someone of the same field as yours. You may fear that they might have a different approach than you on several things, and you might even disagree with them on some of the stuff, but this is precisely what makes this experience beautiful. You got to step out of your comfort zone, explore your options, and know that the other person can be just as interesting as you wish them to be. Don't expect too much from them; after all, it's only a first date, and you don't want to disappoint either them or yourself. Robert Levenson says, "Different personalities may provide couples with complementary resources for dealing with life's challenges."

5. Look presentable, be presentable:

If you want to make a solid first impression and want the person to call you for a second date, you should focus on making yourself look flawless.

From choosing the best outfit that would go with the weather to wearing your favorite scent and making a neat hairstyle, you have to up your game. This will not only impress your date but would also bring you a sense of self-confidence. Hygiene is one of the major things people notice in others, especially when meeting for the first time. Be aware of your body language. No matter how nervous you are, you have to be calm and relaxed in Infront of your date. Try mirroring the movements of your date to show them that you're interested in what they have to say. The study says that the more we are attracted to someone, the more we mimic them. So, make sure you give your date positive signs.

6. Give them the fitting follow-up:

Say your date has been successful. The question arises, what next? Asking them out on another date right then and there might put them in an awkward position, as they didn't have enough time to ponder on this one yet. It could also make you feel like you're rushing things. On the other hand, you might be eager to hang out with them soon because you have felt that connection, the conversation with them flowed smoothly, and you have a ton of things in common. The best you can do is say that you had a great time with them and wish to meet them soon. You can text them after a few days for another date. But try not to sound too desperate and don't expect a reply right away. Maybe, you'll get a text from them to meet even before you're ready for another date. Just hope for the best and be patient.

Conclusion:

Success in life doesn't get handed to you on a silver plate, even if it's related to dating. You have to work hard in this area of your life too. If your date doesn't go as you have planned it to, have no worries, there's plenty of fish in the sea. You could learn from your mistakes and avoid them on your following dates, till you get a perfect one. Learn from the experiences. And if you do get a perfect date, then way to go!

Chapter 3:
6 Ways To Flirt With Someone

No matter how confident and bold we assume ourselves to be, we tend to freeze up and utter a wimpy 'hey' when we see our crush approaching us. Flirting doesn't always come easily to everyone, and there's always struggle, awkwardness, and shyness that follows. But, some people are natural-born flirters and just get the dating thing right.

Knowing how to flirt and actually showing someone that you're interested in them sexually or romantically can be a minefield. But once you get your hands on it, you'll probably become an expert in no time. If you struggle with flirting, we've got some tips to help you master the art of flirting and getting your crush's attention. Below are some ways to flirt with someone successfully.

Be Confident But Mysterious

There's nothing sexier than someone who has a lot of confidence. Of course, I'm not talking about being too overconfident, and it will tend to push people away from you. But if you're strutting down the halls as you own them, your crush (and everyone else) will notice you. Don't give away too much of yourself while being confident. People tend to get intrigued by someone who gives off mysterious vibes. They show their interest in you and avail every opportunity to try to get to know you better. This will lead to you having a chance to make up a good conversation with your crush and even flirt with them in between.

Show That You're Interested In Their Life

Who doesn't love compliments and talking about themselves all the time? We come along with people who mostly like to talk than to listen. If you get a chance to talk to your crush, don't waste it. Ask them questions about their life, get to know their views and ideas about certain things like politics, fashion, controversies, show that you're genuinely interested in them. They will love your curious nature and would definitely look forward to having another conversation with you. This will also give your brownie points of getting to know them better.

Greet Them Whenever You Pass Them

Seeing your crush approach you or simply seeing them standing in the halls can be the scariest feeling ever. You will probably follow your gut reaction and become nervous; either you'll walk past them hurriedly or look down at your phone and pretend like you're in the middle of a text conversation battle. But you have to ignore those instincts, and you have to look up at them and simply smile. You don't have to indulge yourself in an extensive conversation with them. Just taking a second to wave or say hi can be more than enough to get yourself on your crush's radar, as you will come off as polite to them.

Make Ever-So-Slight Contact

The sexiest touches are often those electric ones that come unexpectedly, not the intentional ones that might make someone uncomfortable.

Unnecessary touches can be a turn-on because they signal a willingness to venture beyond the safe boundaries that we usually maintain between ourselves and others. But be careful not to barge into them accidentally. Small, barely-there touches that only the two of you notice are the best. Let your foot slightly touch theirs or lightly brush past them.

Compliment Them

While everyone loves receiving compliments, try not to go overboard, or they would be more likely to squirm in their seat rather than ask you out. You should compliment them lightly about their outfit or fragrance or their features or personality, but keep the subtle flirtation for when the time and moment is right. Giving them compliments would make them think that you're interested in them and want to step up the equation with them.

Look At Them

Experts suggest that we look and then look away three times to get someone's attention. According to the Social Issues Research Centre, maintaining too much eye contact while flirting is people's most common mistake. Our eyes make a zigzag motion when we meet someone new - we look at them from eye to eye and then the nose. With friends, we look below their eye level to include the nose and mouth. The subtle flirt then widens that triangle to incorporate parts of the body. Please don't stare at someone too intensely, or else you'll end up making them feel uncomfortable.

Conclusion

It might seem nerve-wracking to put yourself out there and start flirting, but fear not! It's normal to get nervous around someone whom you like. Follow the above ways to seem confident and pull off a successful flirtation. Know the importance of keeping a balance between revealing your feelings and keeping the person you like intrigued.

Chapter 4:

5 DIFFERENCES BETWEEN CRUSHING AND FALLING IN LOVE

It can be difficult to know the difference between a crush and love. When you meet someone and you are overcome with feelings, how do you know what they mean? It is fairly common for someone to obsess over a new flame and decide that it must be love when, in fact, it could easily be a crush or infatuation.

The first thing to know is that love is a feeling you have for someone but backed up with an emotional connection. It's deeper than a crush, and you will want good things to happen to the person you love. A crush is an intense obsession with someone based on surface information such as looks, a job, or even the fact that you go to the same coffee shop. Fortunately, you can look at the following fundamental differences between crush vs. Love and determine for yourself which one you have.

1. **How long did it take to develop feelings?**

One fundamental difference between having a crush and falling in love is how long it takes to develop feelings. When you have a crush on someone, the feelings come on fast. Sometimes it is called "love at first sight." you meet someone, and you are immediately smitten.

When you love someone, you will develop a deeper emotional connection based on mutual respect and shared values. The only way to know that you share a connection is through shared experiences together.

2. **Do you put the object of your love/crush up on a pedestal?**

Another great factor in helping you determine whether you have a crush or are feeling love (and vice versa) is determining whether you are putting the person up on a pedestal. Is he or she perfect in your eyes? Do you find yourself using superlative adjectives every time you describe him or her? When you have a crush, the other person often appears flawless and the absolute gold standard in relationships.

When you love someone, you don't think in those terms. You love the person for who he or she is, the good and the bad alike. It's more about feeling emotionally safe and connected than it is about being perfect.

3. **How jealous are you?**

Jealousy is a sure sign of a crush. Feelings of jealousy come from a place of not feeling as though you can trust the object of your affection. You should never have to feel that way, and it is a sure sign that it is a crush and not love. When you love someone, you have established a connection that is founded on trust and respect. You will be less prone to irrational thoughts and concerns because your feelings are deeper and more genuine.

4. Are you attracted to other people?

Do you find yourself keeping your options open? Are you drawn to others as well as your new flame? If you find that this is true, you have a crush. It may be exciting and send butterflies through your insides when you have a crush, but it isn't fulfilling. Love is different. You will not even notice if another person is looking at you, no matter how attractive he or she may be. Love leaves you wanting to share fun times and quiet dinners with your one and only.

5. Do you cancel on friends and blow off prior commitments?

When you have a crush on someone, you might find yourself feeling like you have to cancel plans to be available for the person. This is a result of insecurity because a crush is founded in idealism, not in reality. When you love someone, you will never feel pressured to make choices. Your partner will respect you and want you to keep your commitments, and you will not feel as though you have to sacrifice yourself to keep his or her interest.

When you meet someone and start a relationship, it can be hard to know if what you have is the real thing. It can be a bit of an emotional roller coaster, but it will settle down rather quickly if you are meant to be. Having a crush can be a lot of fun, but it is important to nip it in the bud once it runs its course. Knowing the signs of a crush vs. Love can help you make the right choices and move on with your life.

Chapter 5:
5 Signs Someone Only Likes You As A Friend

There's nothing like the feeling of getting friend-zoned by a guy/girl you so desperately wanted to be with. When theoretical physicists started talking about black holes, they were probably referring to the friend zone. You find yourself drooling and crushing hard over them, only to find out that they have never reciprocated those feelings. Spotting the signs that they just want to be friends with you and nothing more is always disappointing. But the sooner you see them, the easier it will be for you to move on.

Sure, it might be a little complex for you at first, as some people tend to be very poor in communicating and can give mixed signals, which might make you confused. It could lead to a bunch of misunderstandings between you two and may also cause you to daydream about them when there isn't anything for you. Here are some subtle signs that they only like you as a friend.

They Never Get Jealous
Overly jealous people can be considered toxic ones, and jealousy isn't always a good thing. But sometimes, in small amounts, it might show that one person does care enough about the other to want them all to

themselves. If the person you like never gets jealous when you're flirting with other people, or when others are showing their interest in you, then it means they don't care about your love life and sees you only as a friend who's having fun. On the contrary, if they show some emotion or are affected by you flirting with others, it might mean they're interested in you.

They Are Always Trying To Set You Up With Their Friends

If you're romantically interested in someone, then it's not a great sign if they're your matchmaker all the time. Relationships might start like this only in the movies, while the reality is different. It's improbable that someone would set up a person they like with their friend or their acquaintance. If they're constantly on your nerve asking you to date people or are being your wing person, then it's a sign they consider you only as a friend.

There's No Flirting From Their

If two people are really into each other and spend most of their time together, then it's nearly impossible for them not to flirt, even if it's a little bit. It's always in their subconscious mind to praise and appreciate someone they like. While some people aren't the flirty type, and some are just straight-up awkward or shy, we can always filter out if they're petrified or just downright ignoring us. If they don't flirt with you ever, like in any way, or if your flirty remarks make them uncomfortable and they reject your attempts straight away, then it could mean that they're not interested in you.

They Discuss Their Love Life With You

Most of the time, people wouldn't gush about their romantic lives in front of you if they seem interested in you. It would simply send out the signal that they aren't available to you. They might talk about their ex-lovers to try to make you jealous or talk about people who are into them to try to impress you, but that's an entirely different kettle of fish. While it can be hard to tell the difference, see if he genuinely seeks your love advice or seems overly interested in someone else. That would mean he likes someone else and not you.

They Rarely Text You Or Asks About You

When someone likes you, they tend to find excuses to text you and talk to you all the time. They might start by asking silly questions that they already knew the answer to, or may indulge in deep conversations with you, or direct the subject elsewhere so that they have a chance to talk to you. They might even ask your friends or friends about you and try to find you when you're not around. On the contrary, if they hardly text you or call you or even don't try to communicate with you, then it's a clear sign that they might not be interested in you.

Conclusion

You should try and be clear about your feelings and ask them to do the same since day one, as it could save both of you from confusion and getting mixed signals and fantasizing about something that doesn't even exist in the first place. You cannot make someone love you, no matter how much you wish you could.

Chapter 6:
8 Signs a Girl Likes You

The human mind is considered one of the most complicated organs, and understanding the female mind can be a hell of a task. In 2017, a professor of neurobiology and behaviour, Larry Cahill, Ph.D., issued the differences between a male and a female mind in his research The Journal of neuroscience. He says that although the total brain size of men is more extensive than women, but a woman's hippocampus, critical to learning and memorization, is more significant than a man's and works differently. The two hemispheres of a woman's brain talk to each other more than a man's do.

Women are fascinating, inspiring, and quite complex creatures. And if you're unsure about the signs that a girl might like you, then you're in it for the long run. Mostly, men are expected to make the first move, like approaching a girl, striking up a conversation, or simply asking a girl out on a date. But women play the lead role in deciding whether a man can initiate romantic advances. They initiate the contact by subtly providing cues if the communication is welcome or not.

It's difficult to decipher a woman's behavior, especially if she's giving you mixed signals. But worry not! we're here to help you see the signs clearly of whether a girl likes you or not. So, save yourself some stress, put your decoder ring on, and let's get started.

Here are 8 signs to know if a girl likes you…

1. She makes eye contact and holds it.

While a lot of people shies away when making eye contact, if you see a girl holding it for more than a fraction of a second (3-5 seconds max), then there's a strong possibility that she's into you. Research says that when you see something that your brain likes, it releases oxytocin and dopamine into your system. These hormones make you feel incredibly joyous. Notice her eyes the next time she makes eye contact with you; if her pupils dilate, then she's definitely interested in you.

2. She laughs at all your jokes (even the lame ones).

When a woman notices a man she's interested in, she would smile, laugh, and giggle more often around him. Even if your jokes are terrible (everyone agrees), but this girl would act as if you're the funniest guy she's ever met. If she counterattacks you with the same humorous and playful banter instead of getting offended, then she's really interested in you. Relationship expert Kate Spring says humor is a sure-fire sign of confidence. And confidence sparks something deep inside women that sets off instant attraction.

3. She mirrors your behavior.

A study published in the Personality and Social Psychology Bulletin proved that subtle "behavioral mimicry" indicates that you're attracted to that person. You might notice that she has adopted your slang, the way that you move your hands while making a conversation, or the pace at which you talk. Jane McGonigal, researcher and author of The New York Times bestseller "Reality is Broken", calls mirroring a love detector. She says, "....the more we feel like we really understand somebody, we're really connecting with them, we're really really clicking with them, the more likely we are to mirror what they're doing physically."

4. **She makes frequent contact with you.**

Instigating conversations can be a lot of hard work for a woman since they expect the opposite gender to start the chit-chat. So, if she's constantly engaging in discussions with you, making efforts by replying to you properly, and getting to know you better, she certainly likes you. Relationship expert Dresean Ryan says, "Believe it or not, something as simple as a good morning text can show someone has deep feelings for you."

5. **She touches you.**

One of the most obvious signs that she's into you is when she touches you. It could be a light brush of her hand against yours, slapping your shoulder playfully, or touching your leg or hair. If she's initiating the touch and does not creep out by yours, instead she seems comfortable with you, then it's a great sign of her being interested in you. According to behavior analyst Jack Schafer, "women may lightly touch the arm of the person they are talking to. This light touch is not an invitation to a sexual encounter; it merely indicates that she likes you."

6. **She gets nervous around you.**

If you're around and she seems to become quiet all of a sudden or starts avoiding you, then know that she's nervous and not uninterested. She might start playing with her hair, rubbing her hands, interlacing her fingers, blink frequently, or compress her lips. If you also notice that her breathing has become ragged and fast when you've entered the room, then that's a lucky sign for you.

7. **She's always available for you.**

Whether you're in a middle of an existential crisis at 3 in the morning or simply want to go for lunch, you text her, and she's at your door the minute after. Even if she's busy, she'll move things around her schedule just to fit you in. You can easily tell by her body language and her behaviors that she loves spending time with you. She's always there for you whenever you need something, going through a bad phase, or enjoying life.

8. **Her friends know about you.**

Women tell their friends everything. And by everything, I mean every single thing. So, if she's confident enough to introduce you to her friends, then consider yourself lucky. If they tease her when you're around or start praising her more in front of you, then there's definitely more to the matter. The approval of family and friends is the most critical aspect in seeing whether the individual cares enough to see a future with you.

Conclusion:

Figuring out if a woman likes you is a very tricky business. You might get silences or mixed signals in the initial few days. But it would be best if you looked for the social cues that women give off when they're attracted to you. Try your best and do not give up, you'll eventually get her!

Chapter 7:
6 Tips To Find The One

Finding someone who matches our criteria can be a difficult task. We always look for a person who is a knight in shining armor. And by time, we make our type. We are finding someone who looks and behaves like our ideal one. We always fantasize about our right one. No matter how hard it may seem to find someone, we should never lose hope. Sharing is always beneficial. And if you trust someone enough to share your life with them, then it's worth the risk to be taken. The person you chose depends upon you only. The advice can only give you an idea, and you have to act on your own.

Now, when looking for someone from scratch can be difficult for many of us. That person can either be the wrong one or the right one. Only time can tell you that. But you both need to grow together to know if you can survive together. And if not, then separation is the only possible way. But if you find the right one, then it will all be good. You have to have faith in yourself. Be your wingman and go after whatever you desire.

1. **Be Patient**

When looking for someone you want to spend your time with, someone you want to dedicate a part of your life to, you have to devote your time looking for the one. Be patient with everyone you meet so you will get to know them better. They will be more open towards you when you give them time to open. Doing everything fast will leave you confused. Don't only talk with them. Notice their habits, share secrets and trust them. They will be more comfortable around you when they think that you are willing to cooperate.

2. Keep Your Expectations Neutral

When you find someone for you, they can either leave you disappointed or satisfied. That all depends on your expectations. If you wait for prince charming and get a knight, then you will be nothing but uncomfortable with them. Keep them neutral. Try to make sure that you get to know a person before passing your judgment.

3. Introduce Them To Your Friends

The people who love you tend to get along together. The first thing we do after finding a competitor is telling a friend. We usually go for the people our loved one has chosen for us. While finding the one is all you. They can play a part in giving advice, but they can't decide for you. When we see one, we want everyone to get to know them.

4. Don't Be Discouraged

You are 30 and still haven't found anyone worth your time. If so, then don't get discouraged. That love comes to us when we least expect it. You have to keep looking for that one person who will brighten your days and keep you happy. Please don't go looking for it. It will come to you itself and will make you happy.

5. Look Around You

Sometimes our journey of finding the one can be cut short when we see the one by our side—someone who has been our friend or someone who was with us all along. You will feel happier and more comfortable with finding the right person within your friend. It will make things much more manageable. And one day, you will realize that he was the one all this time. Sometimes we can find one in mutual friends. They may be strangers, but you know a little about them already. However, finding the one within your friend can save you a lot of trouble.

6. Keep The Sparks Fresh

Whatever happens, don't let your spark die because it will become the source of your compassion. It will make a path for you to walk on with your ideal one. Keep that passion, that love alive. If there is no spark, then you will live a life without any light. So, make your partner and yourself feel that compassion in your growth.

Conclusion

Finding one can be a difficult job, but once we find them, they can make us the happiest in the world. And if that person is honest with you, then there is nothing more you should need in one. You can always change your partner until you find the one because they are always their ones too. You have to focus on finding your own.

Chapter 8:
Confidence: The Art of Humble-Pride

There is a very fine line between confidence and overconfidence, being bold and being belligerent, having authority and having arrogance. It is a line that trips even the most nimble footed, but usually because they have dedicated no clear thoughts on how to manage it. Instead, they follow their gut on how far they can push or how much they should hold back. This is the paradox; you need to be confident. You need self-belief, you need to be assured of your ability and sometimes even certain of what the outcome will be. All of those things are empowering. In the words of Tony Robbins, you have to awaken the giant within. But had Goliath stooped to consider David's sling he would have worn a different helmet. The problem was that Goliath had a belief that he was fully capable of everything just as he was. I like to call it confidence without context, or universal, unanimous support of the self. That is the dangerous kind of confidence that spills over into arrogance. Chess grandmasters will tell you that the moment you assume you will win is the moment you lose. Because that is precisely when you start to make mistakes. You become too focussed on what your next move is that you don't even see theirs. You become so absorbed in your strategy that you fail to account for their plan and the bigger picture. It was confidence without context that made Goliath run straight towards to the flying stone.

Confidence without context is an assumption. And the problem with assumptions is that they go one step beyond the rationality of an expectation. Assumption goes into the fight drunk, having already celebrated the victory. But that leads to its inevitable demise. Expectation remains present, it acknowledges the reality of the situation. Assumption arrives intoxicated, expectation arrives in control. That is the difference. Pride is the greatest antidote to reason, which makes humility its greatest ally. If you want to stay in the fight you need to have both confidence and humility. If you want to stay competitive, if you want to get a promotion, if you want to level up. Whatever it is that you want, I can guarantee that the path to get there is a hopscotch of humility and confidence. Every bold step forward must be followed by a humble one. Note that humility does not take you backwards, it keeps you balanced. You can hop along in arrogance, but you will never last as long or be as strong as the one who keeps an even stride. If you strive for something, then you need to start striding towards it. And the rhythm of your march should beat to the sounds of a two-tone drum. Because confidence without context is like hopping up stairs – you might reach the second floor, but you will never manage the pyramid.

Chapter 9:
The Goal Is Not The Point

If you ever want to achieve your goals, stop thinking about them. I know this goes against everything anyone has ever said about achieving your goals.

Everyone says that think about one thing and then stick to it. Devote yourself to that one single goal as you are committed to your next breath. Check on your goals over and over again to see if you are still on track or not and you will get there sooner than you think.

What I am proposing is against all the theories that exist behind achieving your goals but wait a minute and listen to me.

The reason behind this opposing theory is that we spend more time concentrating on thinking and panning about our goals. Rather than actually doing something to achieve them.

We think about getting into college. Getting a Bachelor's degree and then getting our Master's degree and so on. So that we can finally decide to appear for an interview that we have dreamed about or to start a business that we are crazy about.

But these are not the requirements for any of them to happen. You can get a degree in whatever discipline you want or not, and can still opt for business. As far as job interviews are concerned, they are not looking for the most educated person for that post. But the most talented and experienced person that suits the role on hand.

So we purposefully spend our life doing things that carry the least importance in actual to that goal.

What we should be doing is to get started with the simplest things and pile upon them as soon as possible. Because life is too short to keep thinking.

Thinking is the easiest way out of our miseries. Staying idol and fantasizing about things coming to reality is the lamest thing to do when you can actually go out and start discovering the opportunities that lie ahead of you.

Your goals are things that are out of your control. You might get them, you might not. But the actions, motivation, and the effort you put behind your goal make the goal a small thing when you actually grab it. Because then you look back and you feel proud of yourself for what you have achieved throughout the journey.

At the end of that journey, you feel happier and content with what you gained within yourself irrespective of the goal. Because you made yourself realize your true potential and your true purpose as an active human being.

Find purpose in the journey for you can't know for sure about what lies ahead. But what you do know is that you can do what you want to do to your own limits. When you come to realize your true potential, the original goal seems to fade away in the background. Because then your effort starts to appear in the foreground.

A goal isn't always meant to be achieved as it might not be good for you in the end or in some other circumstances. But the efforts behind these goals serve as something to look back on and be amazed at.

Chapter 10:
Make Time for Your Partner

When I first got into my relationship, I thought my boyfriend and my 100-hour workweek would have to battle it out until the bitter end. Yet somehow, I've managed to maintain both. It turns out there are a lot of weird [ways to make time for your partner](#) when you're busy AF. You may have to get creative and resort to some weird measures, but I am living proof that there is no such thing as being too busy for your loved ones.

We all have to run errands. That time is gone from your workday anyway. So, why not use it to show your partner you care instead of just getting what you need? Picking up each other's shampoo and favorite cereal (or, perhaps more practically, take turns picking up groceries and toiletries for the both of you) is one way to connect without needing to make any more time in your schedule.

You spend the same amount of time cooking for two people as you do for one, but since you're feeding two, you *save* time by doing this. Think about it: Instead of cooking every night, you only have to do it every *other* night. Even if you both eat it in front of your computers, making food for each other is a loving gesture that'll make you appreciate each other.

If you live together, you'll probably be sleeping in the same bed anyway. But even if you don't, your dates can consist solely of sleeping if that's what it takes to make time for each other. Or, if you can't sleep through the night with someone else next to you, you can try just sharing nap time.

Even if you don't get around to working out that much, the time you can devote to exercise will help clear your mind, so it's worthwhile if you can make it out for a short run or yoga class. Plus, [working out together can boost your attraction](#) by releasing endorphins.

I can't always handle this, especially when I need to feel like nobody wants my attention to focus. But for less intensive tasks, it can be comforting to cuddle up to your significant other while you're working. You can even be each other's sounding boards if you need help coming up with ideas.

This one will not work for everyone. But if you have an office in a similar place, your walk or ride to work can be your bonding time, even if it's just part of the way. Even just a shared walk to the train station can pay off if you think ahead enough to coordinate your trips to and from work.

Chapter 11:
First Impressions Matter

Today we're going to talk about a simple topic that I hope will help each and every one of you make a good first impression in every meeting you may encounter in the future.

So why bother with making a good first impression in the first place? The answer is fairly simple - people decide very quickly in the first few minutes whether they think you are someone they might want to associate themselves with or not. They see how you look, how you dress, how you carry yourself, and they decide usually fairly quickly about what label they want to tag on you. Humans are judgemental and superficial creatures by nature. Barring all other aspects of your personality, how you look is the first thing that others can deduce about you.

We have all done this at some point in our lives - we make sweeping remarks about the first "hot guy" or "hot girl" that we see, and we we remark at the way they dress and the choices that they make stylistically. We may find ourself immediately attracted to them based on just their looks.

Of course how we carry ourselves is equally important as well. When we go for interviews, when we meet new clients, the vibes that we let out matters. How others perceive us in that first meeting will set the tone on whether we may be asked back for a second interview, or if our clients will continue to decide on whether to work with us moving forward. Sure if we don't do well in the first impression we may have a chance to redeem ourselves in the second chance we get, but I'm sure that's not where you want to end up if given the choice.

So how can we do our best to make a good first impression in any situation?

I want to start by making sure that you know who your audience is. Do your homework and try your best to anticipate what the opposing party might aspect of you. If you are going for a job interview and you know it will be a formal one, do your best to look smart and dress accordingly. Don't show up with your shirts untucked and un-ironed. Ensure that you look the part of the job you are gunning for. Sure things may go wrong during the interview, but at least you showed up looking like you really are serious about the job and that you want to look presentable for your future boss.

If you know that you are going on a first date for example, make a good first impression by also grooming yourself accordingly to attract your partner. I know it may sound incredibly superficial, but if you look into nature, almost all creatures have a way of attracting their mates. Whether it be through colourful feathers in a peacock, or dance rituals in some exotic birds, or a flowing mane of a lion, all these are ways to catch the attention of their potential partners. When someone dresses nicely it shows that they are making an effort to look good and that they are in the business of winning you over.

Now that I've given you some examples of how looking the part can give you a huge boost in your first impressions rating, I want to move on to the next part which is how you actually carry yourself through the things that you say and the actions that you take.

Everyone knows that a pretty face can only carry you so far if you don't have a good personality to match. Sure we may lust for something that looks good on the outside, but if we take a bite from it and it tastes absolutely gastly, I'm sure most of us would eventually run for the hills afterward. The same goes when you go for interviews as well.

The simplest advice I can give for all of you is to be yourself. Don't try to be something that you are not. In most situations, I believe that staying true to who you are and being congruent in what you say is very important. Yes you have to be professional and do your best to showcase your talents in your area of expertise, but beyond that we do need to try our best to be as authentic as possible. Depending on what our motives are and what we want to get out of the first impression meeting, we have to be really clear about our intentions. If our goal is to deceive, you may find it easy to lie our way through the first meeting, but the truth eventually catches up with us when the opposite party finds that we are not up for job or up to the standards that we have set for ourselves in the first session. If we had stayed true to ourselves from the very beginning, our words will hold more credit and questions to our integrity will be kept to a minimal.

If we want to attract a spouse that is kind-hearted and good-willed, it is only natural for us to expect the same if the opposing party gave us the impression that they are. If it was done out of deceit, over time it will slowly creep up as their authenticity stays to crack and we are revealed their true nature. If we expect others to act and behave the way that is congruent with what they show us in the first impression, we should also do the same for others.

Yes I know that I may be going off a tangent of creating good first impressions. But I am also not going to advocate here that we change ourself completely to make a good impression the first time around only to show up like totally different versions of ourselves the next. I always believe that staying true to who you are is the best way to not only make a good first impression, but also to make a lasting and permanent impression. We want to build a strong reputation for ourselves as individuals who are confident and competent at the same time. We want to earn others' trust not out of deceit but out of skill.

If we find ourselves lacking in certain areas, I propose that we work on it on a consistent and daily basis. If we find that maybe we're not happy with the way we look, make a commitment to get to the gym 5 times a week and to eat healthier. If we find ourselves lacking in key soft skills, we may want to take up a course or go for trainings that help us be better in these areas. If we find ourselves lacking in certain skill sets required for particular job that we want, we may want to consider getting further education so that we are qualified in those areas. The bottom line is, we should never stop working on ourselves. Only then can we truly make a powerful first impression that is credible and lasting.

So I challenge each and everyone of you today to make it a point to put making a good genuine first impression at the top of our list for every new person that we meet. Whatever the reason may be, dress up accordingly and present ourselves well so that we may hopefully get the thing that we want.

I hope you learned something today. Take care and I'll see you in the next one.

Chapter 12:
Don't Overthink Things

Analysis Paralysis, how many of you have heard of this term before? When a decision is placed before us, many of us try to weigh the pros and cons, over and over again, day and night, and never seem to be able to come up with an answer, not even one week later.

I have been guilty of doing such a thing many times in my life, in fact many in the past month alone. What I've come to realize is that there is never going to be a right decision, but that things always work out in the end as long as it is not a rash decision.

Giving careful thought to any big decision is definitely justified. From buying a car, to a house, to moving to another state or country for work, these are big life-changing decisions that could set the course for our professional and financial future for years to come. In these instances, it is okay to take as much time as we need to settle on the right calculated choice for us. Sometimes in these situations, we may not know the right answer as well but we take a leap of faith and hope for the best and that is the only thing we can do. And that is perfectly okay.

But if we translate the time and effort we take in those big projects into daily decisions such as where to go, what to eat, or who to call, we will find ourselves in a terrible predicament multiple times a day. If we overthink the simple things, life just becomes so much more complicated. We end up over-taxing our brain to the point where it does not have much juice left to do other things that are truly important.

The goal is to keep things simple by either limiting your choices or by simply going with your gut. Instead of weighing every single pro and con before making a decision, just go. The amount of time we waste calculating could be better spent into energy for other resources.

I have found that i rarely ever make a right choice even after debating hours on end whether I should go somewhere. Because i would always wonder what if i had gone to the other place instead. The human mind is very funny thing. We always seem to think the grass could be greener on the other side, and so we are never contented with what we have in front of us right here right now.

The next time you are faced with a non-life changing decision, simply flip a coin and just go with the one that the coin has chosen for you. Don't look back and flip the coin the other way unless it is truly what your heart wants. We will never be truly happy with every single choice we make. We can only make the most of it.

Chapter 13:

Ten Signs Your Crush Likes You

The weak knees you get when you see them, the fantastic smell of their cologne that you can't get enough of, the skipping of your heartbeat when you see their smile or hear their laughter, your face lighting up when you see their pictures. Yeah yeah, we know that feeling very well; YOU'VE GOT A CRUSH! It happens to almost all of us. Maybe there's a co-worker who caught your eye or a classmate that you exchange glances. Or perhaps it could be a total stranger that you have just met and pretty soon started liking them.

You keep thinking about them and their dreamy eyes, their pleasant bright smile, their oh so perfectly structured face, and their lips that are so... but wait! Aren't we getting too much ahead of ourselves?

Maybe, just maybe, they've shown some signs too. They say a crush is called so because they leave you feeling crushed if they don't reciprocate your feelings. But if you've wished upon your lucky star and maybe this time, your star took pity on you and have answered your prayer, then your case might become different than the one I just mentioned.

Getting suffocating and thought-provoking mixed signals from your crush might drive you crazy. You are always left wondering, hoping if the indicative signs mean anything. That may be your crush likes you back too. If you are plucking the poor petals of your hundredth rose and enchanting, 'He loves me/He loves me not,' then save it for later, pretty please?

We are here for you, and using our expertise, we will help you figure out if you are your crush's crush too.

Here are ten signs (in no particular order) that will help you analyze if your crush likes you back:

1. **Their eyes are fixated on you:**

They say that the eyes are windows to the soul. A study has found out that people unconsciously fixate their eyes on the things they want the most. People tend to keep eye contact with someone they like, apart from the few shy ones who might not like its intensity; perhaps when you will catch them looking at you, they will look away and blush. But shy or not, you have to notice their pupils. Studies show that an individual's pupil dilates when they see someone they like. They also tend to blink more often while watching their crush. If you feel like you are being stared at by your crush or catches them stealing glances at you, and they smile afterward, then consider yourself lucky. And if he's directly locking eyes while talking to you, then that's just the cherry on top of your sundae!

2. **Notice their body language:**

It is said that actions speak louder than words. Have you ever noticed how you feel around them? Do you get nervous, hyper, shy, or suddenly quiet? Or most importantly, if your crush feels the exact same emotions around you. If he gets flustered or fidgets a little more than usual, or starts to blush or sweat while talking to you, then maybe it's a sign he likes you back. You should also notice that when your crush is standing with you, his feet must be pointing towards you. Weird right? But hey, I don't make the rules. When we are interested in someone, our body naturally leans towards them to be closer. This is a subconscious action that signifies interest. So, the next time you're having a conversation with your crush, notice if he leans in and sits forward with his arms uncrossed, having constant eye contact and listening to you attentively.

3. **They're not afraid to open up to you:**

It's normal to develop trust issues considering we suffer from terrible experiences, like heartbreaks and betrayals, in our lives. We might have built a protective wall around ourselves to keep people from hurting us. But when we are around someone we trust, those walls come crumbling down without us even realizing it. Whether it's about them spending their next vacations abroad, or their future college plans, or maybe their deepest darkest secrets, they don't hesitate to talk about all of it to you. Experts say, vulnerability nurtures attraction and develops a sense of trust by fostering deeper feelings of closeness. So, if your crush is vulnerable and weak around you and does not shy pouring out their heart to you, then you must be someone really special to them.

4. **They want to know a lot more about you:**

From your favorite color to your favorite food, to your favorite book, and even your grandma's birthday! They want to know every single detail about you. They remember the important dates and details of your life, even those that subconsciously slipped out from your tongue. Not only this, they never get tired from hearing about you and asking all about you. They might even watch your favorite tv show or read your favorite book to impress you. They make small gestures from the particulars that you have told them. And they are always looking for more opportunities to get to know you better.

5. **Always willing to help you:**

Men thrive on solving women's problems. I guess it's something biological that men always feel the need to provide for the women he cares about, and vice versa. Whether it's giving her his jacket in the cold or her bringing him warm soup when he's feeling down, it all comes down to how much the individual cares about the other person. Your crush eagerly offers you help with just anything and is always available to lend you a hand whenever you need it. The term 'hero instinct' has been given to men who are always ready to help the women of their liking.

6. **They preen themselves around you:**

As soon as you enter the room, you see them adjust their clothes, sleek back their hair, or touch their face, then know that they are trying to look presentable and impressive in front of you. Preening around the people we like is a subconscious way to advertise our romantic interest. We tend to want to look the best around them. From wearing our best outfits to smelling fresh and pleasant and making efforts to make oneself look attractive.

7. **They become flirty/playful around you:**

Another thing to notice is that if your crush is being flirtatious or funny around you. They might try to get your attention and show affection by being playful in a light-hearted and silly way. They might even call you funny nicknames, tease you, or joke around you. It might also be a sarcastic comment or a light punch on the arm or simply laughing with you on random stuff.

8. **Their friends act weird when you're around:**

If your crush's friends start acting weird when they see you, the chances are that your crush has already told them about you (which, by the way, is basically guaranteed. I mean, who does not say to their friends about their love interest?). Anyways, look for the signs as to how their friends act when you are near them. Do they say their name out loud? Do they giggle or whisper to each other? Do they give you two a playful smile and leave you two alone? Do they randomly start to tell you great things about your crush? Or maybe, they might even ask point-blank if you like the person!

As for you, play along, and maybe their friends would get some sense into them, and they will finally as you out.

9. They try to be always near you:

Do you ever go to a party, hang out with your group of friends, or go to any gathering for that matter but always end up beside your crush? Or perhaps they're making excuses and efforts to see you more often, like a mistaking call or text that results in them asking you out. This might be another sign that your crush likes you; that is, they are trying to get into your proximity. They will try and make sure to spend as much time as they can with you. Whether it's about trying that new restaurant or studying for the English test together, you will see them hovering around you quite often.

10. Their mood changes when you hang out with someone else:

Suppose you are engaged in a deep, meaningful conversation, walking side by side, or just simply laughing with someone from the opposite sex, and you catch your crush feeling gloomy and staring intensely at you both, or walking out of the room, or even joining you guys. In that case, chances are they might be feeling protective or jealous. They want to get all your attention and not share you with anyone else, which is highly adorable. But beware! There is a difference between being playfully jealous and being full-on psychotic possessiveness, which is a huge red flag, and you should probably then stay away from them.

In the end, it is advisable not to assume anything based on just signs and to gut up and tell them how you feel about them. If they reciprocate your feelings, then good for you. If not, then trust me, it'll not be the end of the world; at least you'll be sure of their feelings towards you. And remember, there's always someone out there who would want to be with you. You'll just have to wait and see where destiny will take you.

If you found this video helpful, don't forget to like, subscribe, comment, and share this with someone important to you. I hope you learned something valuable today. Take care, have a good rest, and till the next video ☺

Chapter 14:
The People You Need in Your Life

We all have friends, the people that are there for us and would be there no matter what. These people don't necessarily need to be different, and these traits might all be in one person. Friends are valuable. You only really ever come across ones that are real. In modern-day society, it's so hard to find friends that want to be your friends rather than just to use you.

Sometimes the few the better, but you need some friends that would guide you along your path. We all need them, and you quite possibly have these traits too. Your friends need you, and you may not even know it.

1. The Mentor

No matter which area or field they are trying to excel in, the common denominator is that they have clarity about life and know exactly what their goals are. These people can impact you tremendously, helps you get into the winners' mindset, infuse self-belief and confidence in you then you, too, can succeed and accomplish your goals. They act as a stepping stone for you to get through your problems. They are happy for your success and would guide you through the troubles and problems while trying to get there.

2. Authentic People

You never feel like you have to make pretense around these people. Life can be challenging enough, so having friends that aren't judging you and are being themselves is very important for your well-being. This type of friend allows you to be vulnerable, express your emotion in healthy ways, and helps bring a smile back to your face when you're down.

They help you also show your true self and how you feel. Rather than showing only a particular side of their personality, they open their whole self to you, allowing you to do the same and feel comfortable around them.

3. Optimists

These people are the kind you need, the ones that will encourage you through tough times. They will be there encouraging you, always seeing the best in the situation. Having the ability to see the best in people and will always have an open mind to situations. Everyone needs optimism in their lives, and these people bring that.

"Optimism is essential to achievement, and it is also the foundation of courage and true progress." -Nicholas M. Butler.

4. Brutally Honest People

To have a balanced view of yourself and be aware of your blind spots is important for you. Be around people who would provide authentic feedback and not sugarcoat while giving an honest opinion about you. They will help you be a better version of yourself, rectifying your mistakes, work on your weak spots, and help you grow. These are the people you can hang around to get better, and you will critique yourself but in a good way, helping you find the best version of yourself. Of course, the ones that are just rude should be avoided, and they should still be nice to you but not too nice to the point where they compliment you even when they shouldn't.

Chapter 15:
5 Steps To Using Dating Apps Correctly

There's an old saying that goes like, "You have to kiss a lot of frogs first to find a prince," and these days, it applies to online dating. Does online dating feel like an unsolvable puzzle in your quest for finding 'the one" (or whoever it is that you're looking for)? Then worry no more because you're not alone in this. Online dating is an entirely different ballgame from meeting someone in real life. You have all the information you can get your hands on before meeting them. You may have gone through their short profile or may have exchanged a few words via text or email.

All in all, when you meet someone offline, you may have a lot or very little information about that person ahead of time. As they say, the first impression is the last impression; you have to make sure you apply it both in your online and offline life. Here are some ways to use dating apps correctly.

1. **Choose Your Photos Wisely**

As I've said before, that first impression matters, and nothing can make a better dating profile impression than putting up a great photo. Before setting up your profile, take your time to go through the shots that show off your looks and hint at how your personality is. It would be best if you also kept in mind to post some well establishing shots that your match can use to recognize you when you finally meet them in person. Choose one picture of your close-up face and one more distant snap that shows a complete view of your body. Your features should be visible and don't even think to use an old photo to trick your potential match. We might not be the best judge of our faces, so make sure to ask one or two of your close friends about the pictures you are choosing.

2. Work On Your Bio

A picture may be worth a thousand words, but the bio of your profile is still essential. Even if you are the most charming and loveliest person globally, a blank or a terrible bio will get you nowhere with the people using the apps. Some apps give you enough space to write a complete autobiography, while some limit you to a line or two. No matter what limit or space you get, look deep into yourself and start thinking about your personality and traits that make you different from other people. You should be careful about the areas you should avoid and the ones you should enhance in your profile.

3. Expand Your Expectations

Once you have created a fantastic profile, start looking for partners. Don't be too picky considering the overwhelming number of people using the apps; the possibilities can distract you from the great profiles that are right in front of you. It's normal to find a chance with someone you hadn't considered initially, and it's crucial to venture outside your dating comfort zone. While you should look out for someone with the same opinions and personality as yourself, you shouldn't restrict your options. If you haven't had any luck finding a good match, it may be time to broaden your search terms ad change your criteria. A little flexibility wouldn't do you any harm.

4. Remain Active

You may find yourself getting bored after using the apps for an extensive period. However, it is essential to keep your profile up to date, remember to log in regularly, send messages and run searches, even if you aren't looking for love at the moment. Some algorithms determine what appears on your social apps. So, with every action you take on an app or site, it reveals your preferences and allows you to receive more likely matches. Similarly, if you fail to check the app regularly, it will stop sending the appropriate profiles your way.

5. Make The First Move

If you potentially get your match and hang out with them, make the first move and ask them out. No matter if it's the guy or the girl, if your intentions are clear about the other person, then it shouldn't stop you both from seeing each other. Ask for their schedule and plan a date whenever they're available. Make them feel comfortable first and get them to trust you so they can go out with you without any hesitation.

Conclusion

Bring the fun element into dating apps, and don't just make it seem like you're doing some work. Be patient because things like these take time. Keep engaging and stay positive; you might now meet someone instantly.

Explore your options and then hope for the best. If you need to take a break, do it, and then come back when you're ready to dive in again.

Chapter 16:
10 SIGNS HE DOESN'T LIKE YOU

Is your man as invested in you as you are with him, or does he simply not like you? If you're struggling to decide whether or not he's into you, here are 10 unfortunate signs that he probably doesn't like you.

1. **You have to initiate all of the conversations**

If you only talk to this guy when you make an effort to send him a text, email, or pick up the phone and call him, he might not be that into you. Professional matchmaker kimia mansoor says that when a guy is smitten, he'll want to learn as much as possible about you. Yes, he may be nervous and intimidated by you because he likes you, so you'll make want to make sure that isn't the case first. But if you are making all the effort and he's not even responding, let alone starting the conversations, it might be time to move on.

2. **He doesn't protect you**

A surefire sign that he doesn't like you is if he doesn't protect you against the big and little things in life. Does he make sure you're safe when you cross a busy road? Stick up for you in a verbal argument with someone else? Or put his arm around you when you're feeling vulnerable? There are many ways for a man to protect his girlfriend or wife. The key thing is that he should want to do this because it's built into a man's dna to seek out relationships that allow them to feel like a protector.

3. You notice him flirting with other women in front of you

If your guy hasn't let go of his flirtatious behavior after dating you a few times, it could be that he's not invested in the relationship the way you are. This likely bothers you more than you are letting on, so be honest with yourself about whether or not you think it's okay for him to do that and then make a decision about whether or not to carry on in the relationship.

4. He doesn't seem to care if you flirt with other men

In retaliation for his flirtatious behavior, you start to flirt with other guys, and your man doesn't even seem to care. It could be that he's comfortable with your relationship and trusts you not to cheat, but it's more likely that he doesn't care what you are doing because he's not interested in making this relationship stick. If he's not getting jealous, perhaps he doesn't care enough.

5. He doesn't ask you to hangout

You always have to ask him to do stuff like going to the movies or out to dinner. If every date is your idea and your man doesn't offer any suggestions to hang out or even watch television together on a saturday night, he's already checked out. He might be a relaxed type of guy that doesn't like to initiate, but most likely, he just isn't invested enough to make a time commitment. It's time to move on and give him an ultimatum. Don't waste your time trying to get him to hang out. He might be a relaxed type of guy that doesn't like to initiate, but most likely, he just isn't invested enough to make a time commitment.

6. He's all over the place emotionally

If your guy seems to be hot for you one minute and then ice cold the next, you might be wondering what's going on. Maybe he is not fully over his ex. You're not alone: it's hard for girls to read guys whose emotions are unpredictable. If your guy is not showing up for you consistently, you're probably tempted to find one who can.

7. You can feel like he's not listening

When you are together – which isn't very often – you feel like he's on another planet or has his face buried in his phone. Is he listening? Who knows! But if you feel like he's not, you are probably right. You can try testing him to see if he is, but more often than not, you'll find yourself frustrated with his lack of interest in your conversations.

8. You have no idea who his friends are

A guy who has no interest in continuing a relationship won't invite you to meet his friends. If it's been any length of time and you've heard all about his buddies, but he's never introduced you, be aware: he might not want them to meet you.

9. You can only hang out when it works for him

When you set up a date, he never makes concessions to make time for you and always puts his job, friends, and family first. While that seems noble and loyal at first glance, it's pretty annoying after a while, and you might start to feel like you are not a priority for him in his life. If it is only one time, that's acceptable, but that could become a problem if it is a regular pattern.

1. You don't think he's trying hard to get your attention

Guys like it when girls pay attention to them. If your guy isn't making a fool of himself somehow, at least some of the time to try to get your attention, it might be that he doesn't care if he has it. It's hard to hear, but guys have telltale signs of being into a girl. Wanting to be close and trying to get your attention is always at the top of that list.

Chapter 17: How To Find Motivation

Today we're going to talk about a topic that hopefully will help you find the strength and energy to do the work that you've told yourself you've wanted or needed to but always struggle to find the one thing that enables you to get started and keep going. We are going to help you find motivation.

In this video, I am going to break down the type of tasks that require motivation into 2 distinct categories. Health and fitness, and work. As I believe that these are the areas where most of you struggle to stay motivated. With regards to family, relationships, and other areas, i dont think motivation is a real problem there.

For all of you who are struggling to motivate yourself to do things you've been putting off, for example getting fit, going to the gym, motivation to stay on a diet, to keep working hard on that project, to study for your exams, to do the chores, or to keep working on your dreams... All these difficult things require a huge amount of energy from us day in and day out to be consistent and to do the work.

I know... it can be incredibly difficult. Having experienced these ups and downs in my own struggle with motivation, it always starts off swimmingly... When we set a new year's resolution, it is always easy to think that we will stick to our goal in the beginning. We are super motivated to go do the gym to lose those pounds, and we go every single day for about a week... only to give up shortly after because we either don't see results, or we just find it too difficult to keep up with the regime.

Same goes for starting a new diet... We commit to doing these things for about a week, but realize that we just simply don't like the process and we give up as well...

Finding motivation to study for an important exam or working hard on work projects are a different kind of animal. As these are things that have a deadline. A sense of urgency that if we do not achieve our desired result, we might fail or get fired from our company. With these types of tasks, most of us are driven by fear, and fear becomes our motivator... which is also not healthy for us as stress hormones builds within us as we operate that way, and we our health pays for it.

Let's start with tackling the first set of tasks that requires motivation. And i would classify this at the health and fitness level. Dieting, exercise, going to the gym, eating healthily, paying attention to your sleep... All these things are very important, but not necessarily urgent to many of us. The deadline we set for ourselves to achieve these health goals are arbitrary. Based on the images we see of models, or people who seem pretty fit around us, we set an unrealistic deadline for ourselves to achieve those body goals. But more often than not, body changes don't happen in days or weeks for most of us by the way we train. It could take up to months or years... For those celebrities and fitness models you see on Instagram or movies, they train almost all day by personal trainers. And their deadline is to look good by the start of shooting for the movie. For most of us who have day jobs, or don't train as hard, it is unrealistic to expect we can achieve that body in the same amount of time. If we only set aside 1 hour a day to exercise, while we may get gradually fitter, we shouldn't expect that amazing transformation to happen so quickly. It is why so many of us set ourselves up for failure.

To truly be motivated to keep to your health and fitness goals, we need to first define the reasons WHY we even want to achieve these results in the first place. Is it to prove to yourself that you have discipline? Is it to look good for your wedding photoshoot? Is it for long term health and fitness? Is it so that you don't end up like your relatives who passed too soon because of their poor health choices? Is it to make yourself more attractive so that you can find a man or woman in your life? Or is it just so that you can live a long and healthy life, free of medical complications that plague most seniors by the time they hit their 60s and 70s? What are YOUR reasons WHY you want to keep fit? Only after you know these reasons, will you be able to truly set a realistic deadline for your health goals. For those that are in it for a better health overall until their ripe old age, you will realize that this health goal is a life long thing. That you need to treat it as a journey that will take years and decades. And small changes each day will add up. Your motivator is not to go to the gym 10 hours a day for a week, but to eat healthily consistently and exercise regularly every single day so that you will still look and feel good 10, 20, 30, 50 years, down the road.

And for those that need an additional boost to motivate you to keep the course, I want you to find an accountability partner. A friend that will keep you in check. And hopefully a friend that also has the same health and fitness goals as you do. Having this person will help remind you not to let yourself and this person down. Their presence will hopefully motivate you to not let your guard down, and their honesty in pointing out that you've been slacking will keep you in check constantly that you will do as you say.

And if you still require an additional boost on top of that, I suggest you print and paste a photo of the body that you want to achieve and the idol that you wish to emulate in terms of having a good health and fitness on a board where you can see every single day. And write down your reasons why beside it. That way, you will be motivated everytime you walk past this board to keep to your goals always.

Now lets move on to study and work related tasks. For those with a fixed 9-5 job and deadlines for projects and school related work, your primary motivator right now is fear. Which as we established earlier, is not exactly healthy. What we want to do now is to change these into more positive motivators. Instead of thinking of the consequences of not doing the task, think of the rewards you would get if you completed it early. Think of the relief you will feel knowing that you had not put off the work until the last minute. And think of the benefits that you will gain... less stress, more time for play, more time with your family, less worry that you have to cram all the work at the last possible minute, and think of the good results you will get, the opportunities that you will have seized, not feeling guilty about procrastinations... and any other good stuff that you can think of. You could also reward yourself with a treat or two for completing the task early. For example buying your favourite food, dessert, or even gadgets. All these will be positive motivators that will help you get the ball moving quicker so that you can get to those rewards sooner. Because who likes to wait to have fun anyway?

Now I will move on to talk to those who maybe do not have a deadline set by a boss or teacher, but have decided to embark on a new journey by themselves. Whether it be starting a new business, getting your accounting done, starting a new part time venture.. For many of these tasks, the only motivator is yourself. There is no one breathing down your neck to get the job done fast and that could be a problem in itself. What should we do in that situation? I believe with this, it is similar to how we motivate ourselves in the heath and fitness goals. You see, sheer force doesn't always work sometimes. We need to establish the reasons why we want to get all these things done early in life. Would it be to fulfil a dream that we always had since we were a kid? Would it be to earn an extra side income to travel the world? Would it be to prove to yourself that you can have multiple streams of income? Would it to become an accomplished professional in a new field? Only you can define your reasons WHY you want to even begin and stay on this new path in the first place. So only you can determine why and how you can stay on the course to eventually achieve it in the end.

Similarly for those of you who need additional help, I would highly recommend you to get an accountability partner. Find someone who is in similar shoes as you are, whether you are an entrepreneur, or self-employed, or freelance, find someone who can keep you in check, who knows exactly what you are going through, and you can be each other's pillars of support when one of you finds yourself down and out. Or needs a little pick me up. There is a strong motivator there for you to keep you on course during the rough time.

And similar to health and fitness goal, find an image on the web that resonates with the goal you are trying to achieve. Whether it might be to buy a new house, or to become successful, i want that image to always be available to you to look at every single day. That you never forget WHY you began the journey. This constant reminder should light a fire in you each and everyday to get you out of your mental block and to motivate you to take action consistently every single day.

So I challenge each and every one of you to find motivation in your own unique way. Every one of you have a different story to tell, are on different paths, and no two motivators for a person are the same. Go find that one thing that would ignite a fire on your bottom everytime you look at it. Never forget the dream and keep staying the course until you reach the summit.

Chapter 18:
10 Facts About Attraction

Everything from taking an interest in someone to admire someone physically or mentally is known as an attraction. The attraction could be a romantic or sexual feeling. Attraction can be confusing and takes time to understand. Most of us find it hard to know what we feel about or are attracted to someone. We couldn't figure out what type of attraction it is, but we should remember there is no right way to feel the attraction. There are so many types of attraction, and some could happen at once.

1. **Women attracted to older men:**

So, it is expected that most women these days are attracted to older men just because of their "daddy issues" and the most one is the financial issue but according to study it's not the reason. According to authentic references or studies, the women born to old fathers are attracted to older men, and the women born to younger men are attracted to younger men. As they think that they will treat them just like their father did.

2. **Opposite attraction:**

As we all heard before, "opposite attracts." well, it is true, according to a study of the university of dresden, that both men and women are attracted to different leukocyte antigens, which is also known as the hla complex. A genetic blueprint responsible for the immune function is so unique that this attraction has to do with species' survival. Now, how do our brains detect the opposite hla complex? According to a study, our brain can see the opposite hla complex only by the scents; isn't it a fascinating fact?

3. The tone of women's voices:

According to a study by the university of canada, when women flirt, their voice pitch increases automatically. Not only while flirting, but women's voice tones increase at different emotions. The highest tone of a woman's voice gets when she is fertile or ovulated, and guess what? According to studies, men like the most high-pitched voices of women.

4. Whisper in the left ear:

According to a study, when you want to intimate someone, like whispering " i love you" in their ear, then whisper in their left ear because whispering in the left ear has 6% more effect than a whisper in the right one.

5. Red dress:

Red dress attracts both men and women. It is examined in a study that usually men love women in the red dress. They find it intimidating.

6. **Men with beard:**

Women find men attractive with a beard. Beard with the subtle cut. Another fantastic fact about the beard is that women judged men with a beard to be a better choice for a long-term relationship. This might be because men with beards look more mature and responsible. Beard also makes you look like you have a higher status in society.

7. **Men trying to sound sexy:**

So, women have no trouble whatsoever changing their voice, but men have no clue about it. Women lower their voice pitch and make it sexy, and men find it so attractive, but men find it very difficult to sound sexy. It got a little bit worse when men tried to say sexy. The reason behind this is elaborated in research, according to which men are not focused on making their voice sexy but women do.

8. **Competing:**

Research shows that when you are famous for everyone, and everyone likes them, you get attracted to them and try to get them. You start competing for that person with other people, which makes you feel more attracted to that person. That person will be in your head all the time because you see everyone admiring and chasing that person.

9. **Adrenaline:**

Studies show that adrenaline has to do a lot with attraction. People find others more attractive when they are on an adrenaline rush themselves. According to a study, women find men more attractive when they are ovulating than in another period.

10. **Weights and heights:**

When taking a liking to someone. People always prefer to choose a person who holds the right weight and height according to them. Different people may have different opinions. When they find a person with a likable body, they get easily attracted to them.

Conclusion:

Attraction to someone can play a significant role in getting them. When people are attracted to you, they make you feel worth it all, and you feel ecstatic. Attraction can be=ring in a lot of factors like popularity, relationship and of course, love.

Chapter 19:

Ten Ways Men Fall In Love

Genuine and true Love is so rare that when you encounter it in any form, it's a beautiful thing to be utterly cherished in whatever form it takes. But how does one get this genuine and true Love? Almost every romantic movie, we have seen that a guy meets a girl and, sure enough, falls head over heels for her. But translating that into the real world can be quite a task. The science of attraction works wonders for us. Sometimes we are instantly drawn to some people. On the other hand, we couldn't care less for others. And quite a few times, things flow naturally in our direction, making it all feel surreal and causing butterflies.

A famous psychologist once said: "Love is about an expansion of the self whereby another person's interests, values, social network, and finances become part of your life just as you share your resources with them."

A human mind is, nonetheless, a very complex organ. It can either makes you feel like you're on top of the world with its positive attitude or under it with its negative one. And a male mind, perhaps, seems always like a mystery to us. But it's not such rocket science that we can't get our hands on it. If you're developing feelings for someone and need a bit of guidance to get the man of your dreams to notice you and care about you, then you've just come to the right place!

Here are some ways about what a man needs to fall in Love.

1. Always Be Yourself:

Keeping a façade of fake personality and pretending to be someone you're not can be a huge turn-off for men. Instead let the guy know the real you. Let them see who you really are and what you really have to offer. You will not only gain respect from them, but you wouldn't have to keep hiding behind a mask. If you're pretending to be someone else, that only suggests that you're not comfortable with yourself. And many guys will realize this shortcoming and quickly become disinterested. You don't have to dumb down your intellect or put a damper on your exuberant personality. Men like women who are completely honest with them from the start. Who shows them their vulnerable side as well as their opinionated and intelligent one. You're in no need to pretend that your IQ isn't off the charts. Be your genuine, miserable, confident, and independent self always. That way, he will know exactly what he's getting into.

2. **Make him feel accepted and appreciated:**

From a simple thank you text to calling him and asking him about his day, making small gestures for him, and complimenting and praising him, a man needs it all. Men don't always show it, but they are loved to be told that they look good, they're doing a good job, or how intellectual they are. Sometimes men are confused about where women may stand, and they want to see that he's being supported beyond any superficial matter.

When men share glimpses of their inner self with you and put themselves in a vulnerable position, which men rarely do, this is when it's crucial to make him feel rest assured that he will be accepted and appreciated. If women make men feel lifted high and admired, then it's pure magic for them. His heart will make such a deep connection with you that it can only be amplified from thereon.

3. Listen! Don't just talk:

You would see a lot of men complain that they are not heard enough. And quite frankly, it is true. It's essential to establish a mutual balance in the conversation. Women shouldn't make it all about themselves. They need to let the men speak and hear them attentively, and respond accordingly. Ask him questions about his life and his passion, his likes and dislikes. That way, he'll know that you are genuinely interested in him. Men have a lot to say when you show that you can listen. They'll be more inclined to say the things that matter.

4. Laugh out loud with him:

Men tend to make the women of their liking laugh a lot. When you're laughing, you're setting off chemicals in a guy's brain to feel good. Make him feel like he has a great sense of humor, and he's making you happy with his silly and jolly mannerism. Similarly, men are attracted to women who have a spirit that can make them feel good. Tell him enjoyable stories, roast people with him, jump in on his jokes and laugh wholeheartedly with him. He will become attracted to you.

5. **Look your best:**

You don't have to shred a few pounds, or get clear, glowing skin, or change your hairstyle to impress the men of your liking. You have to be confident enough in your skin! Men love a confident woman who feels secure about herself and her appearance. You don't even have to wear body-hugging clothes or tight jeans to make him drool over you (Of course, you can wear them if you want). But a simple pair of jeans and a t-shirt can go a long way too. Just remember to clean yourself up nice, put on nice simple clothes, wear that unique perfume, style up your hair a bit, and voila! You're good to go.

6. **Be trustworthy:**

Another reason that men instantly attract you is when they have the surety that they can trust you with anything and everything. According to love and marriage experts "Trust is not something all loving relationships start with, but successful marriages and relationships thrive on it. Trust is so pervasive that it becomes part of the fabric of these strong relationship." If you want to win a man's heart, reassure him that he can be vulnerable around you and make him feel accepted and secure.

7. **Don't try to change him:**

"He's completely right for me... if only he didn't dress up like that or snore during his sleep."

Sure we might have a few things on our list about how our partner should be, but that doesn't mean we should forcibly try to change their habits. He might have a few annoying habits that will get on your nerves now and then, but that shouldn't be a dealbreaker for you. Instead, we should accept him with all his wits and flaws. You shouldn't just tolerate his little quirks but rather try to admire them too. If something about him is bothering you, try talking to him politely about it. And he might consider changing it for you!

8. **Have intellectual conversations with him:**

There's nothing that a man finds sexier than women with opinion and intellect. Get his views on a news article, engage him in a heated debate about controversial topics, put your views out the front; even if they clash with his, especially if they conflict with his, he'd be more interested and intrigued about knowing your stance. Show your future partner that you can carry on an intelligent conversation with him anytime he likes.

9. **Be patient:**

I can't stress enough that patience is perhaps the most vital key to getting a guy to fall for you. It would be best if you gave him time to analyze and process his feelings for you. If you tend to rush him on the subject, you might end up disappointed. Even if you do lose your cool, don't let him know it. Just be patient and consistent, and don't come off as too clingy or needy. If you appear too desperate, it's going to turn him off of the relationship entirely.

10. **Let him know you're thinking of him:**

In the early days of dating, you might be hesitant to tell him that you're thinking of him. You love it when he texts you randomly, saying he's thinking about you, so why not reciprocate it? Invest your time, energy, and efforts in him. Leave him short, sweet notes, or text him in the middle of the day saying that he is on your mind or sending him a greeting card with a cute personal message. Don't overdo it by reminding him constantly if he does not respond. None of these screams' overboard' and are guaranteed to make him smile.

Conclusion:

I hope this article deconstructed and gave you some insights into what makes a man fall for a woman. As the saying goes, 'Men are from mars and women are from Venus and Venus is great, but surely, we need to know about the inner workings of mars too.' Just keep the above tips in mind, be consistent and commit to him considerably, and you're good to go! If you found this video helpful, don't forget to like, subscribe, comment, and share this with someone important to you. I hope you learned something valuable today. Take care, have a good rest, and till the next video ☺

Chapter 20:
How To Not Live Your Life In Regret

Today we're going to talk about a simple yet profound topic that I hope will awaken something in you today if you have been sleeping on the wheel of your life. I hope that with this video, I can help you to stop wasting precious time and to keep doing the things that you've always said you wanted to do right now this day. Not tomorrow, but today.

Before we go any further, I want you to write down the things you wish to accomplish before you die. It can be as small as saying I love you to your mom and dad, to something bigger like quitting your job to find something you are passionate about, to leisurely things such as travelling to XXX countries by whatever age. To things such as picking up an instrument that you've always wanted to learn but told yourself you just didn't have the time or that you wont be able to do it, or other things such as making new friends, starting a family, or literally anything under the sun.

I want you to write these things down no matter how big or small, and make them a bucket list of sorts. Many people think that a bucket list is always a leisure thing, but many a times, our bucket list could be more significant in that it is something that we don't just want to do, but need to do.

We may not fill every single thing on that bucket list, but if we can even do half of them, we can say that at least we have tried and we don't regret a single thing. The fact that we attempted is sometimes good enough, it is definitely better than not even trying and living with the guilt of "what if".

Now that we have got this list down. I'm going to jump right into the one thing that will help us put all of this into perspective. And help us truly see what matters at the top of our list. And I think you will be surprised that it may not have anything to do with travel and leisure, but it is the personal goals that we have been putting off.

Are you ready for it?

I want you to close your eyes right now. Find a quiet space where no one will disturb you for the next 5-10mins. I want you to pause this video if you need to at any one point. And I want you to visualise yourself at your deathbed, at the end of your life, whether you see yourself being 80, 90, 100, or even 60 or 70, if you feel that maybe u dont see yourself living a long life. Whatever it may be, I want you to picture yourself in your last moments.

Now I want you to ask yourself, what do you regret not having done in your 20s, 30s, and 40s. What is that one thing that you just couldn't live with yourself having not done, and what that greatest regret may be. Was it not committing your life to helping others, was it not pursuing your passion? Was it not being a good father, mother, child, friend, lover? What is it? Who do you see around you? Are there any friends that are there to see you off? Are there any family members, cousins, loved ones there? Or have you not been a good person that none of them are there to see you? Are you lonely or surrounded my love? Are you happy that you've kept your word and done the things you said you would? Or do you regret not trying?

Do you feel like your heart is full because you have conquered every experience that life has to offer? Or do you regret not spending enough time outside seeing the world for what it truly is? Do you regret not moving to a country that you said you would one day, and just lived to see people live their best lives vicariously through Instagram and Facebook and YouTube? I want you to be as honest as you can with yourself about your current actions and project them forward into the future. Are they going to bring about the kind of peace that you would feel at the end of your life knowing you've done everything you possibly can and without regret?

Take some time to think about the things I said and see if you can paint a vivid picture of what they is like. Did you commit to eating healthily that you can see yourself living to a ripe old age? Or are you consuming junk food everyday that you can't even realistically see yourself being healthy past the age of 50?

As you are visualising these, I want you to write down any thoughts that passed through your head as you see these images. Are there any new priorities that you didn't know existed? Any shift in your bucket list? Anything that jumped out to the front of the queue that you need to fix right this second? or to start doing right now?

If you are done I want you to open your eyes. How did that feel? Was it a surreal feeling to imagine yourself dying and looking back on your life, your teens, your 20s, your 30s. What were your biggest regrets and biggest accomplishments?

I want you to take this bucket list with you and take action on them. If you can prioritise them according to practicality, do it. If there are some easy tasks that you want to execute in next 6months, I want you to start them now. If your goal is to make some new friends that you can take to your golden years, I want you to start searching for them now so that you don't end up old and alone. Being lonely is one of the worst things that can happen to you, and I dont wish that on anyone. If you need to build up some friendships, dont waste time, because friendships takes time to nurture, and you don't want to end up in a situation that you don't have anyone to look for support, comfort, and simple companionship as you grow old.

I challenge each and everyone of you to live your life to the fullest, to live a life without regret, and that starts by taking action on the things that matters the most. It is not always about becoming a millionaire or a billionaire, because money can't buy everything. Money can't buy friends, it can't buy companionship, and it will not last. Build and create things that you can take with you right up to your death bed. And Remind yourself that life is short and not worth wasting.

Today we're going to talk about a topic that hopefully helps you become more aware of who you are as a person. And why do you exist right here and right now on this Earth. Because if we don't know who we are, if we don't understand ourselves, then how can we expect to other stand and relate to others? And why we even matter?

How many of you think that you can describe yourself accurately? If someone were to ask you exactly who you are, what would you say? Most of us would say we are Teachers, doctors, lawyers, etc. We would associate our lives with our profession.

But is that really what we are really all about?

Today I want to ask you not what you do, and not let your career define you, but rather what makes you feel truly alive and connected with the world? What is it about your profession that made you want to dedicated your life and time to it? Is there something about the job that makes you want to get up everyday and show up for the work, or is it merely to collect the paycheck at the end of the month?

I believe that that there is something in each and everyone of us that makes us who we are, and keeps us truly alive and full. For those that dedicate their lives to be Teachers, maybe they see themselves as an educator, a role model, a person who is in charge of helping a kid grow up, a nurturer, a parental figure. For Doctors, maybe they see themselves as healers, as someone who feels passionate about bringing life to someone. Whatever it may be, there is more to them than their careers.

For me, I see myself as a future caregiver, and to enrich the lives of my family members. That is something that I feel is one of my purpose in life. That I was born, not to provide for my family monetary per se, but to provide the care and support for them in their old age. That is one of my primary objectives. Otherwise, I see and understand myself as a person who loves to share knowledge with others, as I am doing right now. I love to help others in some way of form, either to inspire them, to lift their spirits, or to just be there for them when they need a crying shoulder. I love to help others fulfill their greatest potential, and it fills my heart with joy knowing that someone has benefitted from my advice. From what I have to say. And that what i have to say actually does hold some merit, some substance, and it is helping the lives of someone out there.. to help them make better decisions, and to help the, realise that life is truly wonderful. That is who i am.

Whenever I try to do something outside of that sphere, when what I do does not help someone in some way or another, I feel a sense of dread. I feel that what I do becomes misaligned with my calling, and I drag my feet each day to get those tasks done. That is something that I have realized about myself. And it might be happening to you too.

If u do not know exactly who you are and why you are here on this Earth, i highly encourage you to take the time to go on a self-discovery journey, however long it may take, to figure that out. Only when you know exactly who you are, can you start doing the work that aligns with ur purpose and calling. I don't meant this is in a religious way, but i believe that each and every one of us are here for a reason, whether it may to serve others, to help your fellow human beings, or to share your talents with the world, we should all be doing something with our lives that is at least close to that, if not exactly that.

So I challenge each and everyone of you to take this seriously because I believe you will be much happier for it. Start aligning your work with your purpose and you will find that life is truly worth living.

Chapter 21:

10 TIPS TO STOP LIKING YOUR CRUSH

Very often, people experiencing a major crush know their expectations are unrealistic. They may even be aware that they don't have a chance with this crush. Maybe it's incompatibility. Or maybe the other person is taken. One thing's for sure: it can feel heartbreaking and all-consuming. If you want to know how to get rid of a crush and stop obsessing, it's important to consider the situation in objective terms. So what do you do if you find yourself caught up in a crush? Below are some ideas on how to get rid of a crush:

1. **Talk to them**

Find out if you have anything in common. Ask what's going on in their lives. As mentioned above, you might be surprised to find that their personality is nothing like you'd imagined it to be. You may even find that you disagree on important topics, or that they're intellectually lacking which can lead you to being over your crush.

2. **Do not avoid your crush**

In doing so, you may keep the fantasy alive. You owe it to yourself to have a real conversation with them. You may find there is no chemistry between the two of you and decide to move on.

3. Get busy with other aspects of life

You had a life before meeting this person, and that life continues despite your feelings for him or her. Get back to that life, and focus on the things that bring you joy. Distractions that you find fulfilling can take your mind off of your crush and remind you that you have a lot going for you with or without this person in your life. Focus on your education, your work, volunteering for a charity, or even learning a new hobby. Don't over exert yourself while trying to get to know your crush.

4. Spend time with family and friends

 surrounding yourself with the people that mean the most to you-people who love and respect you for you--can remind you that you are whole, with or without a partner.

5. Confide in your loved ones about your crush

They may surprise you with a great piece of advice. For instance, a parent or aunt might share why they think you have a crush on this person and what that says about you. Or perhaps they have had their own experience with a crush and can impart some words of wisdom about how to handle the situation. Perhaps you have dating patterns that you don't see, and they can shed some light on your choices. Maybe this new perspective on your love life could help you figure out how to move on.

6. Question yourself about the origin of this crush

Take the emphasis off of him or her, and focus on yourself. Why do you feel this way? Could there have been other circumstances that led to the crush? Maybe you were feeling down the day you first met, and your crush smiled at you at the right moment? Sometimes, feelings can be situational, and when that person becomes an actual part of our lives, we may feel differently.

7. Take a look at the reality of the situation in its entirety

is this a fantasy relationship that you've created in your mind? Ask yourself, "does this person have the qualities of the person i want to be with? Or am i projecting them onto him or her?

8. Give yourself a chance to grieve

If you do believe, after trying all of the above, that you've missed out on your true love, give yourself space to feel sad about it. Acknowledge and sit with those feelings; don't ignore them or bury them because this will only lead to unresolved feelings that you'll have to address down the road. Or if you've determined that your crush was just that--a crush--allow yourself to grieve the feelings that were there. You probably spent a good amount of time fantasizing, and that can be fun and exciting. When the fantasy ends, it can be jarring and uncomfortable.

9. Stop following them on social media

You do not need reminders of him or her or updates about what he or she is doing every minute of the day. Furthermore, most people only post the best of what's happening in their lives, so you will likely not be looking at the full picture.

10. Lastly, the most fun option

Put yourself out there to remind yourself that there are plenty of other people who want to date you. You can join an online dating site, ask your friends to set you up, or join a club that explores one of your interests. All of these are great ways to meet new and interesting people.

Chapter 22:

7 Signs You Have Found A Keeper

Are you looking for Mr. or Mrs. Right? Or do you think you have found the right person, but how can you be sure? Sometimes, we meet someone who seems like the person you would want to spend your whole life with, but during those times, someone is in for a quick hookup. The only partners worth keeping are the ones that give you the positive vibes that you need after a dull and tedious day, the ones that make you feel happy, and your relationship doesn't feel boring at all. Here are signs that you have found a keeper.

1. **They inspire you to become a better person:**

When we meet someone very kind, helpful and overall a friendly person that person usually inspires us to be better and luckily the world is full of friendly people. Is your partner like this too? Is he warm, kind, and helpful? Does he inspire you to become a better version of yourself? Then you know you have found yourself a keeper. You know you have found the right person when your partner works hard, gives you and his family time, and has his life organized.

2. **They are always there:**

There are times when we all suffer when things get tough to handle. At times like these, a person always needs support and love to get through the hard times. If your partner is there for you even when you can't defend yourself and they cheer you up, you know that this is a keeper. A perfect partner is someone who knows how to make you laugh even when you are crying, your partner will never believe the things people talk about behind your back, and he would never hesitate to lend you a hand when you need some help.

3. **They know you more than yourself:**

Sometimes it fascinates us how someone can know us more than we know ourselves; it feels perfect when someone knows how or what we are thinking. If your partner knows what you are feeling without telling them, then they are the one. Does your partner know what you are comfortable with? Can they tell when you feel upset? Do they motivate you to do better and ask you to chase after your dreams? If so, then don't waste more time thinking if this is the right person for you because it is.

4. **Your interests are common:**

Sure, opposites attract, but too many differences are not usually suitable for someone's relationship. It would help if you had a common interest with your partner, like having common beliefs, values, and religious perspectives. When you agree on these things, your bond will become more robust, and you would find it very easy to live with that person.

5. **They are honest with you:**

Finding an honest person is a tiring thing to do; many people lie more than twice a day, but how can that affect your relationship? The right one may lie about small things that don't matter that much, like whether the color suits you or not; they may say those things to make you feel good about yourself, but lying about other things like financial status, health, or fidelity can be more serious. A true keeper would never keep these things from you, and they would always be honest with you even if the truth upsets you.

6. **They don't feel tired of you:**

Although everyone needs some space, even from the person they love the most, he will never get tired of you if he is the one. Your partner will never feel bored with you; on the contrary, your partner will never get tired of looking at you, admiring you, being with you, and above all, love you. When a person is so in love with you that they want to spend every second of their life with you, then you know you have found a keeper.

7. **You are a part of their dreams:**

Can your partner not even imagine your life without you? Has your partner already planned his future, and you are a big part of it? If so, you know that this one's a keeper. You both have reached a point in your lives where even thinking about living without each other sounds absurd, and then you know that you have found a keeper.

Conclusion:

A keeper is someone that loves, cherishes, and cares for you like no one has ever had. Don't worry if you haven't found your keeper, and it is just a matter of time before you do because, for every one of us, there is someone out there.

Chapter 23:
Never Giving Up

Today I'm going to talk about a topic that I feel very inspired to share. In recent times, never giving up has helped me to push through the initial failures that I had experienced when it came to my career which I later found traction in. I hope that the story today will inspire you also do the same.

It Is all too easy for us to give up when the going gets tough. Starting something new is always much easier but sticking through it and grinding through all the problems that you will most certainly face, is the greater challenge on the road to success that many of us are not willing to put ourselves through.

In recent years, I have had many occasions that it was my persistence that actually yielded the fruits of my labour 2-3 years after I had begun the journey. Success was not found immediately.

A few years ago, I began my online career to make money and I found a new business that I was interested in. I invested time and money into it and found some success in the beginning. I gave up all prior aspirations to pursue a traditional career to embark on this journey and I had nothing to lose.

However after 2 years pouring my heart and soul in this venture, I faced a tough reality when something happened to my business and I lost everything. I lost my sole stream of income and I felt absolutely lost, not to mention crushed that all my time had literally gone up in smoke. I started to doubt myself and question why I even bothered embarking on this path in the first place. I really did not know what to do and had no Plan B. I spent the next few months wandering about trying to figure out what's next. At one point I did feel like giving up and going back to finding a regular job despite knowing that that is something I really did not want to do.

After months of exploring, I decided that I would give my first venture another go. I created a new account and began the journey again, from scratch. I faced many obstacles that were not there before and the struggle was terribly real. I felt pressure from myself to make it work because I felt that there was nothing I was really good at. I needed to prove to myself that I wasn't a failure and that fire lit up inside me to be successful at it at all cost.

To put it simply, eventually my persistence did pay off and I managed to build back some of the income stream that I had lost with new strategies that I had employed. What I only realised much later was that it was actually my experience having been in the business for two years prior that helped me navigate this new strategy much quicker. Everything was done at lightning speed despite the obstacles and I was astounded by the pace in which it picked up. It was in that moment that I understood the principle of never giving up. Because if I had, I would have literally flushed away all the time and energy I had invested earlier in the business down the toilet. It was my attitude of never giving up, and learning from my mistakes that got me through the second time around.

Another story that I want to share about never giving up is something much simpler, and it had to Do with something that happened around the house. In a random event, somehow my door got jammed by an appliance around the house. And no matter how hard I tried to push it simply wouldn't budge. After cracking my head for hours, together with my parents, we still couldn't figure out how to get the door to open no matter how many things we tried. At one point my dad decided that the only way was to break down the door. However the persistence in me didn't want to give up. I found a strategy that could possibly work, involving a knife, and long story short I managed to get the door to open with a great deal of strength. In that moment I felt like the king of the world. Never giving up and persisting felt like the greatest feeling on Earth. And it got me fired up to want to apply this same persistence to all aspects of my life.

It was with these joint experiences along with many others that gave me the conviction that solidified the principle that I have been hearing from gurus every single day about never giving up. That only when you had given up have you truly failed. And I believe every single one of those words today.

So I challenge each and everyone of you today to try this out for yourself. To go back to something you have decided that you had called quits on and to give it one more try. Use your expertise, use your experience, learn from your mistakes of what went wrong before, modify the new plan, and try again. You might be surprised at the outcome. Never ever give up because it's never really over until you have decided to quit.

Thank you, I hope you learned something today and I'll see you in the next one.

Chapter 24:

How to Love Yourself First

It's so easy to tell someone "Love yourself" and much more difficult to describe *how* to do it. Learn and practice these six steps to gradually start loving yourself more every day:

Step 1: Be willing to feel pain and take responsibility for your feelings.

Step 1 is mindfully following your breath to become present in your body and embrace all of your feelings. It's about moving toward your feelings rather than running away from them with various forms of self-abandonment, such as staying focused in your head, judging yourself, turning to addictions to numb out, etc. All feelings are informational.

Step 2: Move into the intent to learn.

Commit to learning about your emotions, even the ones that may be causing you pain, so that you can move into taking loving action.

Step 3: Learn about your false beliefs.

Step 3 is a deep and compassionate process of exploration—learning about your beliefs and behavior and what is happening with a person or situation that may be causing your pain. Ask your feeling self, your inner child: "What am I thinking or doing that's causing the painful feelings of anxiety, depression, guilt, shame, jealousy, anger, loneliness, or emptiness?" Allow the answer to come from inside, from your intuition and feelings.

Once you understand what you're thinking or doing that's causing these feelings, ask your ego about the fears and false beliefs leading to the self-abandoning thoughts and actions.

Step 4: Start a dialogue with your higher self.

It's not as hard to connect with your higher guidance as you may think. The key is to be open to learning about loving yourself. The answers may come immediately or over time. They may come in words or images or dreams. When your heart is open to learning, the answers will come.

Step 5: Take loving action.

Sometimes people think of "loving myself" as a feeling to be conjured up. A good way to look at loving yourself is by emphasizing the action: "What can I *do* to love myself?" rather than "How can I *feel* love for myself?"

By this point, you've already opened up to your pain, moved into learning, started a dialogue with your feelings, and tapped into your spiritual guidance. Step 5 involves taking one of the loving actions you identified in Step 4. However small they may seem at first, over time, these actions add up.

Step 6: Evaluate your action and begin again as needed.

Once you take the loving action, check in to see if your pain, anger, and shame are getting healed. If not, you go back through the steps until you discover the truth and loving actions that bring you peace, joy, and a deep sense of intrinsic worth.

Over time, you will discover that loving yourself improves everything in your life—your relationships, health and well-being, ability to manifest your dreams, and self-esteem. Loving and connecting with yourself is the key to loving and connecting with others and creating loving relationships. Loving yourself is the key to creating a passionate, fulfilled, and joyful life.

Chapter 25:
6 Relationship Goals To Have

We live in a generation where the term "relationship goals" has become a part of the trendy vernacular. It may seem more like a hashtag than anything else, but we all are eager to go into the depth of its meaning. A beautiful photo of a stunning couple having a good time together? Relationship goals. A cute text message sent to a girlfriend from his boyfriend? Relationship goals. A perfect wedding? Relationship goals. All these might seem sweet and enviable and look like an absolute dream, and it doesn't mean that these come off as accessible to them. If you have ever been in a relationship, you would know exactly what I'm saying.

Love is not always fireworks, passion, and butterflies. Relationships are not just date nights, kisses, and cuddles. And love is not that glamorous as it looks on social media. But when you strive to build something together, involving your selflessness, commitment, and even sweat and tears, those are actual relationship goals. Here is a list of what relationship goals you must have with your partner.

1. **Always Do New Things Together**

Sure, alone time might be great, but together time is where the magic happens too. Avoiding your relationship becoming mundane and a rut, you both should try to do new things together. This could be choosing any vacation spot or having an exciting adventure together. You both should make a list of all the things you want to do with each other and keep adding stuff that might pop later. Tick things off as you go, and you'll never run out of things to do together.

2. Be Each Other's Biggest Supporters

Perhaps one of the best things about being in a relationship is that you'll always have someone in your corner. Regardless of how crazy or unrealistic your dreams and goals may sound, your partner should be your biggest supporter. Seeing the person you love believing in could come off as a massive motivation to achieve your goals. This goes both ways; both men and women need to feel emotionally supported. You both should take some time out to discuss what emotional support looks like to you, what and when you need it, and then provide the said support for each other.

3. Put Each Other First

Putting each other first in your relationship will ensure that you're paying attention to each other's needs and making sure they are being met. You have become selfless with each other, and you both strive to make each other happy and would do anything to put a smile on each other's faces. You complement each other, protect each other, support and love each other, no matter the obstacles or circumstances.

4. **Know The Importance of Alone Time**

As much as you don't want to keep your hands off your partner in the early stages of your relationship, it's essential to know that you both need time alone to recharge and refill your cup. Spending all of your time together isn't sustainable, and alone time is significant. It will help you maintain your individuality, allow you breathing space, and encourage a closer relationship with each other when you spend time together.

5. **Keep The Physical Connection Going**

Sex isn't always an option when dealing with different phases of your relationship. There are going to be times when it might not be physically or mentally possible. But this in no way means that you should stop all physical connections. Physically touching the person you love releases an oxytocin hormone; this feel-good love hormone reduces stress and makes you feel wonderful things. You can stay physically connected by holding hands, cuddling, or simply leaning on one another.

6. **Speak Positively About Each Other**

Speaking ill of your partner with others is not only disrespectful to them, but it's also disrespectful to your relationship. Sure, you can vent in tough times, but make sure you talk about the actions and behaviors that upset you and not their personality traits. Always speak positively and kindly of each other. Even if their behavior irritates you, focus more on the characteristics you love of them and let it pass.

Conclusion

Relationships are complicated but beautiful at the same time. As simple as the above factors may sound to you, these things take a lot of effort and hard work to be implemented. But when you do all of these with the person you love the most in the world, then all of it can be worth it.

Chapter 26:
9 Signs an Introvert Likes You

A lot of people out there are conscious to know about the tell-tale signs that reveal if an Introvert Likes You or not. You are probably unsure if someone you know has a secret crush on you and you are eager to find out so that you can reciprocate those feelings, or maybe you want to be find out - out of mere curiosity.

Well, I want to first say that because there are many different kinds of introverts, we may not be able to cover all aspects of it. Some introverts like to be alone in their own comfort zones while others like to hang out with their inner circle of close friends and relatives. But basically an introvert is generally shy and more reserved by nature. They are usually more quiet and may seem like they have built up a little wall around them in the initial meetings you have with them.

In today's video, we are going into 9 specific signs than an Introvert Likes You. Hopefully this will shed a brighter light on this topic and bring you some lightbulb moments. So without any further delay, let's get right into it.

Number one
They will Try to Open up

Introverts are shy creatures that look for soul connection like a meeting of minds. So when an introvert likes you, they will try to open up, they will try to share their thoughts and feelings with you. They will tell you about that one best day of their life and they will tell you how they feel about themselves asking you, do you feel the same way?

So if an introvert overshares with you then you can take it as a plus point as they don't tell these things just to anyone. They tell you these things because you are special to them and they want you to share your world of thoughts too.

Number two

They Know A Lot About You

You might be amazed at this one and might be thinking, how can an introvert know that much about me so quickly? Ahmm, never underestimate their researching skills, just saying. If an introvert likes you then they could potentially look you up on social media, they might check out your posts to get to know who you are as a person a little more. They do their own behind-the-scenes search because they may be too shy to ask you in person, or they might do so to feel that they feel like they may know more about you before committing to liking you. So if they know these little details about you then there is a high chance that they do indeed like you.

Number three

They Will Be First To View Or Like Whatever You Post On Social Media

This one also comes under the previous point. If an introvert likes you, they might be the first to like your post on social media because they may be too shy to message you directly or tell you in person that they find you interesting. An introvert will leave breadcrumbs behind to show that they are interested in you. So yeah, you gotta check if they are doing it or not.

Number four
They Look At You More Than Usual People

If an introvert likes you then they will surely check you out. Whenever they come in front of you or if you are sitting in a group then that introvert will look at you like more than once, without making you feel uncomfortable. Yes! They have this talent. So if you catch them looking at you, then they are probably into you.

Number five
Laughing Nervously

If an Introvert likes you then they might shutter or blush in your presence as well as laugh nervously. They can also get tongue-tied while talking to you. Want to know the reason? Let me tell you. When an introvert talks to you, they are actually out of their comfort zone, so that's why they appear hyper-alert. They are putting themselves out there. Give them the space to be themselves if they appear to be acting this way.

Number six
Immediately Answer your Call Or They Call You

Introverts generally don't like taking calls. It would not be wrong to say that they let all calls go to the voicemail unless it's the call from their food delivery guy. So if an introvert picks up your calls or calls you to talk to you then they might be head over heels over you.

Number seven
Inviting You To Hangouts

Here, I would go back to the first point where I said, introverts don't share their private world with a normal person. Introverts don't go out much but still, they have some favorite places like a coffee shop, a park that makes them feel good, or a hiking trail. So if an introvert takes you to these kinds of places, it means they want to share some part of what makes them feel good.

Number eight
They Step Out Of Their Comfort Zone

This is the most that an introvert can do for you. Do you imagine how difficult it is to step out of your comfort zone? Not everyone can do it except for the person who likes you unconditionally. So if an Introvert likes you, they would love to go to parties, or in a music festival only if they know you would be there. They can stay up late at night just to talk to you and to spend some time with you.

Number nine

Writing "Love Messages"

Now, you might be thinking if a person writes us a love letter then it's an obvious thing that they like us, how is it a sign then? Let me tell you how. Actually, an introvert's love message is different from others. They write things like, hey, how are you? How's your day going? Now, these things are common for an extrovert, they can ask these things to anyone but for an introvert, these messages are like love letters. As you know, introverts don't like talking much face to face so they explain their feelings by writing you a letter or sending you a text.

And writing is the apple pie of introverts. In writing, they can explain how they feel about you without being deficient of words but they will not do it. Introverts!! So if you are getting this kind of message or letters from an introvert, then it's an obvious thing that they like you.

So that's it, guys, we are done with our today's topic of nine Signs an Introvert Likes You. Now, it's time for you to share your thoughts. What do you think about these signs? Have you got your answer yet or not? And if you are an introvert then let us know if there are some additional things to help others. If you got value from this video then smash the like button and don't forget to subscribe to our channel as we will be talking about some amazing topics in the future. See you soon!

Chapter 27:
6 Signs You Are Ready To Move To The Next Step In A Relationship

If you're dating someone long enough, chances are you might know them well now and are ready to take your relationship to the next level. You both work out well together through all the ups and downs, connect with each other, and make each other's life wonderful. So whether you're thinking about making your relationship official by introducing them to your family and friends, moving in with them, or even getting engaged, it can both be scary and exciting when you think about making the relationship serious and taking that leap of faith.

If you feel that you have a healthy relationship, you can't imagine your life without your partner and are in a good place emotionally, then say no more. Here are some signs to convince you that you should up your game!

1. You Both Trust Each Other Fully

Being able to trust someone entirely isn't as easy as it sounds, especially in times like these and the world we're living in right now. The most significant quality one can look for in a partner is how much they value our trust. If you are confident that your partner will always have your back and you can be weak and vulnerable in front of them, maybe you should consider taking the next step. If you have told something to them in confidence and they don't share the information with anyone, and likewise if you do the same, then you both are fortunate.

2. You Support Each Other Through The Good and Bad

Having someone by your side who you know would always support you, no matter what is nothing short of a blessing. Your partner has always comforted and consoled you through the negative phases and cherished and cheered you through the positive ones. Even if they were dealing with their problems, they made sure you were okay first. Most of the time, we tend to emotionally drain out or become frustrated by being there for people. But with your partner, you are always ready to lend a helping hand and even an ear, listen to all of their problems and shortcomings and support them every step of the way.

3. You Both Apologize To Each Other When Needed

One of the major signs of a toxic relationship is when your partner doesn't apologize or take accountability, even if they know they are wrong. These relationships tend to have a dead end. You might have noticed that your partner admits when wrong and apologizes, even if not straight away; they do it sooner or later. They try to sort out the arguments and fights calmly and try to listen to your point of views and opinions too, instead of forcing theirs on you. They make sure that you're okay after the fight and may even make small gestures to make you feel that they are guilty and you are more important than any of the arguments you both get into.

4. You Give Each Other Space

You both have a level of freedom and independence both within and outside the relationship. You both aren't on each other's throat and nerves every second. You both have different hobbies and passions that you pursue. You both can meet your friends alone or hang out by yourself, without stressing over if your partner would mind. This is a sign of a healthy relationship when you don't keep buzzing your partner with unlimited calls or texts, ask them about their whereabouts, or cling to them all day.

5. You're On The Same Page With Them

Even if you and your partner don't share the same goals, hobbies, dreams, passions, or even the same views and opinions, you're still on the same page with them about your values and future. For example, both of you have discussed either having children or no children in the future, getting a destination wedding or a simple one, moving out of the city or across the country, or settling in the same spot where you both are right now. Agreeing on the same stuff shows that you both prioritize the same things and are compatible with stepping up your relationship.

6. You Feel Safe With

One of the signs that your relationship is ready for the next step is the feeling of comfort and security when you are with them. You can be your utter authentic self with them without fearing that they might judge you or dislike you. You have shown all of your sides to them, the good and the bad, and they still love you regardless. They like your quirks and don't get annoyed or irritated by your behavior. You also have accepted your partner's flaws and imperfections and still look at them the same way.

Conclusion

Taking the next big step in a relationship could be confusing and stressful, especially when you find yourself confused and unclear. So if you have found someone worthy of your time and energy, don't let them go. Instead, cling onto them, and make efforts to keep your relationship floating.

www.ingramcontent.com/pod-product-compliance
Lightning Source LLC
LaVergne TN
LVHW020448070526
838199LV00063B/4877